I Am
Your Puppy

This is my book. I will teach you how to care for me after you bring me home. You will find more facts about me in these bubbles throughout the book.

I Am
Your Puppy

By Gill Page

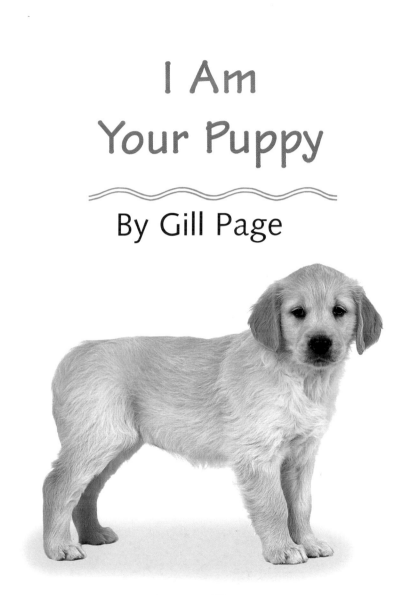

WATERBIRD BOOKS

The Author

Gill Page has been involved with a wide variety of animals for many years. She has run a successful pet center and has helped rescue and find homes for unwanted animals. She has cared for many animals of her own and is eager to pass on her experience so that children may learn how to care for their pets lovingly and responsibly.

Mc Graw Hill Children's Publishing

This edition published in the
United States of America in 2004 by
Waterbird Books
an imprint of McGraw-Hill Children's Publishing,
a Division of The McGraw-Hill Companies
8787 Orion Place
Columbus, Ohio 43240-4027

www.MHkids.com

Library of Congress Cataloging-in-Publication Data is on file with the publisher.

© 2000 Interpet Publishing Ltd.
All rights reserved.

Credits

Editor: Philip de Ste. Croix
Designer: Phil Clucas MSIAD
U.S. Editors: Joanna Callihan and
  Catherine Stewart
Production Editor: Lowell Gilbert
Studio photography: Neil Sutherland
Colour artwork: Rod Ferring
Production management: Consortium,
  Poslingford, Suffolk CO10 8RA

Printed in Hong Kong.

ISBN 0-7696-3391-9

1 2 3 4 5 6 7 8 9 10 IPP 09 08 07 06 05 04 03

~ 4 ~

Contents

Dogs have been living with people for about 12,000 years.

Making Friends

Hello. I am your new friend. What is your name? I would like you to give me a short name. That will make it easy for me to remember. I will tell you lots about myself in this book so that you will know how to take care of me. I am very smart. You will be amazed at all the tricks I can learn. When I am young, I will be tired after we have played together. Put me into my nice warm bed when I am looking sleepy. My mother kept me clean by licking me. You will have to brush me to keep my fur clean and shiny.

I use the whiskers on my nose to help find my way in the dark.

Please don't leave me alone for too long. I like being with people. All the games we play will make me hungry. Will you remember to give me my meals when you have yours? I will need a bowl of water when I am thirsty. I will have to wear a collar and leash when we go out. I know we are going to have lots of fun together.

Getting To Know Me

I have rough hair. My friends have all sorts of different fur. Some have short hair and others have long, silky, or curly hair, just like people. If I am a purebred puppy, you can look at my mother and father and you will see what I will look like when I grow up. It will be harder to guess how I will look when I am older if I am a crossbreed, which is a mixture of different breeds.

When I wag my tail it means I am happy.

I have four paws, a cold, wet nose, ears that may stand up or flop down, and a tail that may be short or long. My fur can be white, brown, black, red, gray, or yellow, or it can be a mix of colors. I may have spots of color or large patches. If you want to pick me up, put one hand under my front legs and the other hand under my bottom. If I keep wiggling when you are holding me, please put me down so that I do not fall. I need a lot of exercise. I will not be happy just sitting around the house. Please think carefully before you choose me. You will want to be sure that I am the right pet for you and your family.

Taking Me Home

A puppy like me will be happy living with you and playing games. Some of my friends are too big, too wild, or too noisy to live in your home. Your parents should ask a veterinarian or other pet expert which breed of puppy will live happily in your house.

When you take me home, please let me see where I am going.

When you come to choose a pet, take a good look at me and all my brothers and sisters. I will be the one that comes to greet you and wants to play with you. I will be bouncy and happy. I should have a cold, wet nose and bright, shiny eyes. My fur must be clean and dry, even around my bottom. I must be at least eight weeks old before you take me home. When you come to pick me up, bring a pet carrier with you. I like the ones that have a wire front so that I can see where I am going. A blanket in the bottom will make it nice and cozy.

My First Day
At Home

I know that I will be very happy living with you, but I will miss my brothers and sisters at first. You probably missed your family when you first went to school. Cuddles and lots of love will make me feel better. Keep me in one room until I have settled down. I will need a quiet corner that is just for me. I can take a nap there after we play games. You can keep my bed there. I will be out of your way so you won't accidentally step on me.

My cuddly toy comes to bed with me.

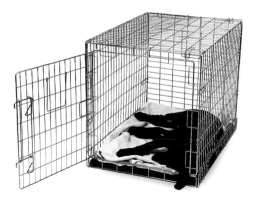

Do you have any other pet friends living with you? I want to meet your other pets when you are there to help me get to know them. Don't leave us alone together in case we fight. Grown-up cats and dogs can be scary. When everyone goes to bed, shut me in my wire cage. Put a hot water bottle under my blanket, but be sure it is not too hot. The heat will feel like my mom. A clock ticking near me will help to make me feel sleepy. I will need my bowl of water, too. Leave some toys with me so I can play until you get up in the morning.

If I am frightened, all the hair will stand up on my back. This is called "putting my hackles up."

Toilet Training

One of the lessons I have to learn is how to be clean and not make a mess in your house. Every time I eat, drink, or wake up, please take me outside so that I can go to the bathroom. Or, you can train me to go on newspaper at first. When I go to the bathroom in the right place, tell me I am a good dog. You can use a phrase like "Let's go outside!" and I will soon learn what you want me to do.

Shouting at me if I make a mess only frightens me. You see, I don't really understand what you are saying. I may have accidents that you will have to clean up. Use rubber gloves and a cloth with some warm water and disinfectant to take the smell away. If the spot still smells, I will think that it is the right place to use and may go there again.

When I first come to live with you, I will have to go to
the bathroom a lot. If I wake up in the night, your
parents will have to let me out. When I
go out for walks, you will have to clean up after me, too.
I should not leave messes in public places.

Time For Bed

Do you have a nice bed to sleep on? I would like a cozy bed, too. When I am little, buy me a solid plastic bed. I like a cushion or blanket to lie on. It makes my bed softer and warmer. The blanket or cushion will need washing every week. It might get smelly and full of fleas if you don't do this. Put my bed into my wire cage. If you leave the door open in the daytime, I can go to bed whenever I am sleepy.

Do you take a teddy bear or doll to bed with you? I like to take some of my toys to bed with me. I like the toys that I can chew. My bed should have sides to it, or it should stand on legs. I really do not like sleeping in a drafty area. When I have grown up and stopped chewing on things, you can buy me a bean bag. I can really snuggle down in that.

My Favorite Foods

I will eat all sorts of things, even foods that are bad for me. Before you bring me home, ask what I have been eating. If you buy the same food for my first few meals, I will not get a stomach ache. I will need special puppy food until I get older. It has nutrients in it that will help me to grow big and strong.

I can eat dry food or canned food.

Wait until I am four months old before giving me canned food. It can upset my stomach if I have it too soon. I need to have a bowl of fresh water near me, because I can get very thirsty. When I am one year old you can feed me other kinds of food. Vegetables and eggs are good for me, and I can finish up any healthy food you have left. Remind me not to beg for food when you arc cating, but please give me my meals when you have yours.

I do not have to eat only meat. I like vegetables, too.

Meal Times

It is hard to tell you how much food to give me because
we puppies are all different sizes. Weigh me and then
look at the instruction on the bag or can to see how
much I will need. You can feed me kibble (dry) food or
canned food. Crunching on kibble will keep my teeth
clean. It will also exercise my jaw. Whatever you choose,
make sure it is made especially for puppies. If you are not
sure what to feed me or how much, ask my breeder or
the veterinarian for advice.

Only put my food in my special dish.

Feeding Schedule

- **2-6 months old:** Three to four meals a day.

- **6–10 months old:** Two to three meals a day.

Dogs that are less than 90 pounds (40 kg.) at full maturity can switch to adult dog food when they are 12 months old. Puppies that will weigh more than 90 pounds (40 kg.) should transition to adult dog food when they are about two years old. Ask your vet to be sure you are feeding me the right food when I reach maturity.

The best food and water bowls for me are the heavy ones that I can't knock over or push around the floor. Please keep them clean. I don't like it when they are smelly.

Treats and Tidbits

Do you like sweets? I love my treats, but I must not eat yours. Salt and chocolate can make me very sick. You can help your mom or dad make some treats for me. Cut or tear up pieces of bread and then ask your parent to cook the bread very slowly in the oven until it is hard. I can crunch up the bits when they are cold. This is good for my teeth.

That looks really tasty, and you say that it is also good for my teeth. I did sit when you asked, so may I eat my treat now?

My favorite treats are chews. You can buy them at the store. I can chew them for a long time. That makes my teeth feel good. Don't buy chews that are shaped like shoes when I am little, as I might get confused and chew your shoes by mistake. Never give me cooked bones or small raw bones. Small pieces can break off and get stuck in my throat. The knuckle end of a nice beef bone is good for me to gnaw on, so ask the butcher for one. Tasty little treats can help when you are teaching me things. Give me a treat when I follow your command. Do not feed me too many though, or I will gain too much weight.

Playtime

I enjoy playing with my toys and playing games. Playing helps to make me fit and strong when I am young. Even when I am a grown-up dog, I can still play games with you. If you and I play ball games in the yard, we must be careful around the plants so that we do not get in trouble. The smallest ball I should play with is a tennis ball. I can choke on or swallow anything smaller. Playing in the park with a flying disk is good fun for both of us.

These are good doggy toys. I can play with them for hours.

I like squeaky toys. There are some toys that you can
hide treats in for me to find. I can play with those for
hours. Throw a toy for me, then call me back. If I bring
the toy back and give it to you, I have learned to fetch.
We can have a game of tug-of-war with a dog pull, but I
will have to learn to let go of the toy when you say
"drop." Watch me to make sure I don't chew my toys
into little pieces and swallow them.

Looking My Best

There are all sorts of different brushes and combs that you can buy to keep my fur looking neat and clean. If I have short hair, it is easy to keep it free of tangles. A bristle brush or rectangular slicker brush is the easiest to use. Please do not brush me too hard, though. You might make my skin sore. It will feel the same as when somebody brushes your hair roughly or tugs at the tangles. My friends that have long hair will need wide-toothed brushes and combs. They need to be brushed more often. Keep my brushes clean, and throw away any old hair.

My fur will look good if you use these brushes to groom me.

In winter a sweater like this one will keep me warm.

I will molt (shed some of my coat) twice a year.
I have less hair in the summer when it is hot, and
I grow extra hair in the winter to help keep me warm. I will need to be brushed more often at these times. If it is very cold, I may need to wear a sweater to stay warm when we go for walks. I could wear a waterproof coat if it is raining. Choose one that fits me snugly, but that is not too tight. I still want to be able to run around.

How To Groom Me

I am covered in hair and I need your help to keep it looking good. When you brush me, start at my head and brush backwards to my tail. Don't miss any spots, please. Reward me with a treat when you have finished. Some of my friends, like poodles, do not molt, so every six weeks they will have to be taken to be groomed. Some terriers will also need special trimming at the beauty parlor.

Brush me the same way my fur grows. It tickles if you brush it the wrong way.

*When you wash me, be careful not to
get soapy water into my ears or eyes.*

Remember to check the fur between my toes. It can get matted there, too. Ask a grown-up to trim the hair from my toes with scissors. If I have very long hair, I will need a lot of brushing every day. Sometimes I get smelly and need a bath. You will need help to wash me. Use water that is just warm, not too hot or too cold, please.

I don't like getting water in my eyes and ears. Use a shampoo made for dogs, or a baby shampoo, and rinse it out well. Rub me with towels to dry me off.

*Please try
to brush me at least
once a day. It will help
to keep me healthy.*

Collars and Leashes

I need to get used to wearing a collar as soon as possible. Put one on me while we are playing games and I will soon forget about it. At first, take it off at night and when you are leaving me alone so that I don't get caught on something. As I grow up, you can leave my collar on all the time. When you fit it on me, leave enough space to get at least two fingers between my neck and the collar. I will probably try to scratch my collar off! Clip the leash onto the collar for a short time while we are indoors. I will be used to it when we go out for walks.

Slipping two fingers under my collar shows that it is not too tight.

There are many leashes and collars to choose from.

Teach me to walk properly on the leash and I will not need to wear a choke chain or halter. An extending lead lets me run around safely while you still can keep hold of me. Many communities have laws that require pets to wear leashes in public areas. Talk to your local police department or animal control office to find out what the laws are in your area.

Learning How To Behave

I need to know how to behave properly. You will have to teach me. There are four important words I need to learn. These are *sit*, *heel*, *stay*, and *come*. You will have to say each word very clearly and show me what it is you want me to do. I don't really understand language. I just learn that certain words mean I must do certain things. One person should teach me at first. That way I won't get confused.

Please don't shout at me or hit me when I get things wrong. I don't understand what you are saying. If you see me doing something wrong just say "no" and ignore me for a while. A few short lessons every day, with lots of praise and treats, will help me learn quickly. Every dog, from the tiniest to the largest, can learn to be well-behaved.

When I am six
months old, we can
go to dog training
classes together. We will
learn how to do all sorts
of new things there.

Training me
shows that you are
the boss at home –
not I.

Basic Training

Sit Put your hand on my back, in front of my back legs, and very gently push down. Say "Sit" at the same time. Reward me with a pat and a treat. Do this two or three times a day until I learn what you mean.

Heel When I am used to the collar and leash, I can learn to heel. Have me walk by your side. If I tug ahead, gently pull me back and say "Heel." If I keep tugging, tell me to sit and then start again. When I do it correctly, reward me with a treat.

Stay Use a long leash. Tell me to sit. Hold your hand up, take a few steps backwards, saying "Stay" to me at the same time. If I sit still, come back to me and praise me. Walk further away. Soon, you will be able to make me stay even without my leash.

Come Do the same as for "Stay," but when you are a few steps away, call my name and say "Come." Give me lots of praise and a treat when I do it right. Then, I will always want to come when you call.

If you train me well, you could enter me in a dog show.

Keeping Fit and Healthy

My doctor is called a *veterinarian*, or *vet* for short. My vet will help to keep me fit and healthy. Before I can go out for walks, the vet must give me shots to keep me from catching diseases. I have to have shots every year for as long as I live. I may have some tiny worms living inside my stomach. The vet will give you medicine for me that will kill the worms. The vet will also check me for fleas. There are some drops you can put on my fur to kill the fleas. The vet will tell you how to do it.

I am going to visit my vet. He will check me over carefully and make sure that I am fit and healthy.

The vet can also inject a microchip under my skin.
This stores information about me. If I ever get lost, any
vet or rescue center will have a machine that will be able
to read the microchip and find out who my owners are. If
I am not eating properly or don't want to go for walks,
always take me to the vet right away for a check-up.

Fleas can bite
you as well as
me.

If I Have Puppies

When I am six months old, the vet can spay or neuter me. Girl dogs are spayed and boy dogs are neutered so that they do not have puppies. You may think it would be fun to have puppies, but would be a lot of hard work. It would cost a lot of money, and you would have to find good homes for all the puppies.

We are so good when we are asleep.

I am only one day old, but my mother carried me inside of her for about 62 days before I was born.

If I have puppies, I will lick clean and dry each puppy as it is born. I need to be with them in a warm box or bed so they will not get cold. At first, their eyes are closed and they cannot hear. I will care for them and keep them clean until they go to new homes. I need extra food while I am feeding the puppies with my milk. When they are three weeks old, you can begin giving them extra food. When the puppies begin walking around, you can start to pick them up and hold them.

How to Write a Report on Your Pet

You may choose to write a report about your pet for school. Start by making an outline of what you would like to say about your pet. The outline should begin with an introduction and end with a conclusion. In between the introduction and the conclusion, you should list three or four characteristics about your pet that you would like to write about.

In the introduction, state your topic, which is your pet, and you should tell the reader what you will be discussing in the rest of your report.

After the introduction, provide the reader with a more detailed description of your pet's characteristics. For instance, you may want to talk about your pet's appearance, your pet's favorite toys, and your pet's quirky mannerisms. Cover these topics in separate paragraphs in your report.

After you finish the detailed description of your pet's characteristics, you should give a short summary of your whole report. Then, you may want to end your report with a funny story about your pet. When you are finished, you will have a wonderful record of your pet that you can return to in years to come.

Puppy Checklist

1. Give me food and water every day.
2. Wash my food bowls every day.
3. Exercise and train me every day.
4. Brush me and check my eyes, ears, and paws every day.
5. Look in my mouth every day. Are my teeth clean?
Do I have any scratches or bleeding?
6. Weigh me every week.
7. Wash my blanket and bed once a week.
8. Check and treat me for fleas once a month.
9. Check with the vet about when I should receive
heartworm medicine.
10. Write down the date for my yearly booster shots and
put it somewhere you can see it

Playing It Safe

Check your house for dangerous things before you take me home. Make sure that cords and other things I should not chew are out of my reach. Block the stairs off so that I do not try and climb them. I might fall. Check the yard and make sure there are no places where I can get out. Ask a grown-up to look for poisonous things that I might eat. Slug pellets and car anti-freeze can kill me if I eat them. Make sure that I cannot fall in a pond or a swimming pool as I might drown. Keep me in the house if your parents are mowing the lawn or moving the car.

There are lots of rules and laws about keeping dogs. Your parents should ask the vet or local police station for more information.

A "pooper scooper" is a clean and easy way to pick up my mess.

I am not allowed to leave any messes in public places. You must pick up any messes I make. Throw the mess away in a garbage can, or take it home in a plastic bag to get rid of it.

Never leave me in the car. If it gets too hot or cold, I could die.

My Relatives

I will be either a purebred or a crossbreed puppy. Some breeds are not really suitable as family pets. Very tiny dogs, ones with lots and lots of fur, or those that have been bred as guard dogs are best not to have. Medium-sized dogs like Labradors, Golden Retrievers and Cavalier King Charles Spaniels make good family pets. Crossbred puppies can be any size. They are usually very healthy. Look at my paws. If they are really big, I will probably grow up to be large. There are often a lot of crossbreed puppies at rescue centers that need good homes.

Flat-coated Retrievers love to splash around in water.

Purebred puppies cost more, but you will know what they will look like when they grow up. Whatever puppy you choose, you know that we will always love you and will be a part of the family for many years.

A Note To Parents

The relationship between child and pet can be a special one. We hope this book will encourage young pet owners to care for their pets responsibly. Studies show that developing positive relationships with pets can contribute to a child's self-esteem and self-confidence.

It is essential to stress that parents also play a crucial role in pet care. Parents need to help children develop responsible behaviors and attitudes toward pets. Children may need supervision while handling pets and caring for them. Parents may need to remind their children that animals—like people—need to be treated with love and respect.

In addition to a happy and suitable home, all pets need food, water, and exercise. Being a pet owner can be a costly and time-consuming experience. Before choosing a pet, be certain that your family's lifestyle is conducive to the type of pet you wish to own. Talk to a local veterinarian if you have questions.

Owning a pet can provide a wonderful opportunity for children to learn about responsibility, compassion, and friendship. We wish your child many years of happiness and fulfillment with his or her new pet!

The smallest dog weighs about 2.21 lbs. (1kg.) and the largest 185 lbs. (84kg.).

Acknowledgements

The author and publisher would like to thank the owners who generously allowed their pets to be photographed for this book and the children who were models. Specifically, they would like to thank Harriet de Freitas, Florence Elphick, Tracy Clark, Zip, Mike, Joanna, and George Greenstreet, Tom, Mrs Illius, Duff, Pogo, and Simon Paterson, Spotty, Marie Puryer, and Bertie. Thanks also to Denis Blades of Gattleys, Storrington, Steyning Pet Shop, Neil Martin of Washington Garden Centre, Washington, Rolf C. Hagen (U.K.) Ltd., Interpet Ltd., and Farthings Veterinary Group, Billingshurst.

Thanks are due to the following photographers and picture libraries who kindly supplied photographs that are reproduced in this book.
Marc Henrie: 3, 6, 13, 29, 35 lower, 36, 37, 39, 45 lower, 48.
RSPCA Photolibrary: 7 (Mark Hamblin), 8 (Cheryl A. Ertelt), 12 (E.A. Janes), 18 (Steve Cobb), 31 lower (Angela Hampton), 38 (E.A. Janes), 44 (Cheryl A. Ertelt), 45 upper (Alan Towse), 46 (Angela Hampton).